Bartering Days

by Marianne Lenihan

Scott Foresman
is an imprint of

PEARSON

Glenview, Illinois • Boston, Massachusetts • Mesa, Arizona
Shoreview, Minnesota • Upper Saddle River, New Jersey

Katie wants to learn to play the violin. Tina wants to learn to ride a bike. If they agree to teach one another these things, then Katie and Tina have bartered.

Bartering is trading goods, **knowledge**, or services with others. Barterers simply trade what they have for what they need.

Bartering began thousands of years ago, before money was used. Farmers traded crops for cloth to make clothes. A blacksmith might have shoed the horse of a **merchant** in trade for an item from the merchant's store.

This merchant has beads to barter.

    Sometimes one person would have to trade several small things for one big thing to make the trade fair. Suppose a **carpenter** has a big table. A **carpetmaker** wants it. The carpetmaker might have to trade three or four small rugs for the big table.

Neighbors often joined together to trade. They built houses for new neighbors or barns for **straying** animals. Each neighbor knew that his or her work would be rewarded someday when he or she needed help.

This woman is offering bread to trade for shoes.

American colonists and Native
Americans traded for what they wanted
and needed. Native Americans had
plenty of furs to barter for the cloth,
thread, and tools of the American
colonists.

Bartering is also a way for a family to save money. Instead of using money to buy items or services, families may barter for what they need.

Dad	Mom	Daughter	Daughter
knowledge of how to start a small business	bread machine	exercise equipment	collection of sports cards

This way, they can keep their money in the bank and still get what they need.

A family's bartering plan might look like this, once they have found another family to barter with them.

Items or Services to Be Traded

Dad	Mom	Daughter	Son
carpentry work	food processor	tutoring in math	bike and skateboard

The Jones Family

Today, people barter in many ways. Bartering partners can be found on the Internet and in newspapers and magazines. They can be found in your neighborhood.

A community theater company needs to advertise its summer plays, but it doesn't have enough money. It does have an entire floor of empty offices.

Businesses barter with other businesses. What might bartering look like in the **marketplace**? Here is one example.

A local radio station needs office space. It will run ads for free for anyone who can provide office space.

SOLUTION: The community theater barters its office space for free advertising on the radio station.

To understand bartering better, a
class of third graders decided to have a
"Bartering Day" with their teacher's help.
The students each brought one item to
school that they no longer wanted.

12

On Bartering Day, each student showed his or her item. The students then decided what they wanted to barter for.

Most students found items they wanted. Some made several trades before they were finished bartering. Others decided to keep their own items.

The next time you decide to trade an
item or a chore, think about its value and
the value of what you might be trading for.
You might decide to wait for a better offer.

Before you decide to barter anything, check with your parents! Your parents will know the value of almost everything in your house. They will know whether it's OK for you to barter something. Once you have permission, have fun bartering!

Glossary

carpenter *n.* someone whose work is building and repairing things made of wood.

carpetmaker *n.* a person who makes carpets and rugs for floors.

knowledge *n.* what you know.

marketplace *n.* a place where people meet to buy and sell things.

merchant *n.* someone who buys and sells goods for a living.

plenty *n.* a full supply; all that you need; a large enough number or amount.

straying *adj.* wandering.

thread *n.* a very thin string made of strands of cotton, silk, wool, or nylon, spun and twisted together.